CONTORTION, GERMAN WHEELS,
AND OTHER MIND-BENDING

CIRCUS
SCIENCE

BY MARCIA AMIDON LUSTED

Consultant:
Vesal Dini, PhD in Physics
Postdoctoral Scholar at
Tufts University
Center for Engineering Education Outreach
Medford, Massachusetts

CAPSTONE PRESS
a capstone imprint

Title: Contortion, German wheels, and other mind-bending circus science / by
  Marcia Amidon Lusted.
Description: North Mankato, Minnesota : Capstone Press, a Capstone imprint,
  [2017] | Series: Edge books. Circus science | Includes bibliographical references and
index. | Audience: 4 to 6.
Identifiers: LCCN 2017012462
ISBN 9781515772828 (library binding)
ISBN 9781515772866 (eBook PDF)
Subjects: LCSH: Acrobatics—Juvenile literature. | Circus
  performers—Juvenile literature. | Circus—Juvenile literature.
Classification: LCC GV1817 .L86 2017 | DDC 791.3—dc23
LC record available at https://lccn.loc.gov/2017012462

Editorial Credits

Abby Colich, editor; Heidi Thompson, designer; Kelly Garvin,
media researcher; Laura Manthe, production specialist

Photo Credits

Alamy: Hans Blossey, 17, Larry Lilac, 5, Piero Cruciatti, cover, Ros Drinkwater, 29; Getty
Images: Andrew Chin, 20-21, Dan Porges, 23, Didier Messens, 18, Kristian Dowling, 25;
Newscom: MIKE SEGAR/REUTERS, 13, picture-alliance, 14, WILL BURGESS/
REUTERS, 8-9; Shutterstock: CHEN WS, 26, Hung Chung Chih, 6-7, testing, 10-11

Artistic elements: Shutterstock: 21, benchart, Gun2becontinued, Igor Vitkovskiy,
mikser45, Milissa4like, Nimaxs, Roberto Castillo, s_maria, Supphachai Salaeman

Printed In the United States of America.
010364F17

TABLE OF CONTENTS

Mind-Bending Acts of the Circus!

Welcome to the circus! Take your seat! We're about to begin! Here you'll see mind-bending acts of all kinds. Acrobats dance in the air. Contortionists bend their bodies. Performers climb and stack themselves into pyramids. Right before your eyes, the seemingly impossible becomes possible.

Circus acts amaze and entertain audiences. Some acts are funny. Others make you hold your breath. Every circus act also features something else. It's something very important — an opportunity to understand how the world works by looking at the science behind the acts!

DO NOT
TRY THIS
AT HOME

Circus acts are a blast to watch, but DO NOT try them yourself. Performers spend years training. They practice every day. Performing a circus act without the proper training and correct safety precautions could result in serious injury. Instead, simple activities that you CAN TRY are included. They will help you understand the science behind the circus. They are safe, easy, and fun!

HUMAN PYRAMID

Shh! The circus is starting! You can't wait to see what's first. Six performers enter the ring. They line up shoulder-to-shoulder. Then they get down on their hands and knees. Moments later, five more performers climb on top of them, getting on their hands and knees as well. More performers enter and climb atop the others until they form a perfect triangle with their bodies. The audience stares in awe at this human pyramid.

How come the performers aren't crushed by the weight of those above them? The pyramid relies on **weight distribution**. When one person climbs on top of two people, his or her weight is mostly balanced evenly between the two people below. This means that each person on the bottom is only holding up half the weight of the person directly above. As the pyramid grows taller, the weight distributes to more people, with those in the middle holding up more weight than those on the sides.

DON'T
TRY THIS AT HOME

TRY THIS INSTEAD

If you step on one paper cup, what happens? You smash it! What happens if you step on several at one time? Let's find out. Grab two cardboard squares, about 2 x 2 feet (60 x 60 centimeters) each. Place one cardboard square on the ground. Cover it with paper cups all face down. Place the other cardboard square on top. Very carefully step on top of the cardboard, one foot at a time. Did you crush the cups? That's equal weight distribution at work!

CIRCUS FACT
The world's tallest human pyramid was built in India in 2012. It was 44 feet (134 meters) tall.

weight distribution—the spreading of weight among available supports

ADAGIO

What's next? You wonder anxiously. Then one performer, known as a base, enters. She lies down on the floor. She raises her arms, facing her palms upward. Another performer, the flier, climbs onto the base's palms. Her arms are outstretched to her sides. She looks like a graceful flying bird. They continue to move together. The base stands, sits, crouches, and lies down. She holds up the flier, who balances on her hands, thighs, and shoulders. These adagio performers almost seem to be dancing.

How can the base hold up the flier without dropping her? The key is adjusting to each other's **center of gravity**. The center of gravity is the balancing point in an object, due to how its weight is distributed. If the flier moves, her center of gravity moves too. The base must also change position to match the shift in weight. For complete balance, the center of gravity of the flier must be directly above the center of gravity of the base. Otherwise, the flier will begin to topple over. The performers spend weeks practicing their movements to make sure they stay balanced during the act.

HOOP
JUMPING

The last act was great, but this one is sure to amaze. You see metal hoops stacked vertically on top of one another. A performer runs out, does a flip, and soars upward through the top hoop. He lands on his feet on the other side. Immediately, another performer runs out, flips, and jumps through the top ring too. A series of performers run, flip, and jump high through the hoop. The audience ooh's and ahh's.

How can these performers jump so high? When the performers come out on stage, they don't walk. They run. Running gives them horizontal **speed**. As they jump, they redirect their horizontal speed into vertical height. They plant their feet right before jumping. Their planted feet are a launching point, allowing some of the horizontal **momentum** to be transferred into vertical momentum. The faster they run, the more vertical momentum they will have.

Technique is important too. The performer must rotate his body in just the right way, or else he will touch the hoop, which could result in a fall.

speed—a measurement of how fast something is moving
momentum—a measure of an object's straight-line motion, calculated as a product of its mass and velocity

BANQUINE

The stage is empty. Then three performers quietly walk out onto the floor. Two of them, called porters, face each other. They clasp each other's forearms. Then the third performer, a flier, climbs onto the platform created by the interlinking arms. She balances herself, then jumps and flips through the air. The porters catch her as she comes back down.

This banquine performer seems to defy **gravity**. How does she do it? Newton's laws of motion can help us understand. Sir Isaac Newton was an English scientist who lived from 1643 to 1727. He identified three laws about motion. The first law states that an object at rest will stay at rest, and an object in motion stays in motion unless an external **force** acts on it. The flier is at rest until the porters throw her into the air, exerting a force on her. She **accelerates** upward, and she would keep moving upward if it weren't for another force acting on her: gravity. Gravity brings her back down into the arms of the porters.

Newton's second law of motion is at work too. It says that the heavier an object, the more force required to change its motion. The amount of force the porters need to throw the flier in the air depends on how much she weighs.

Newton's third law says that every action has an equal and opposite reaction. The porters must be very strong. As they push the flier upward, the flier pushes back with equal force, so porters must hold themselves steady against the ground so as not to accelerate backward.

CIRCUS FACT

Banquine may remind you of a cheerleading routine. It uses many of the same basic moves.

gravity—an attractive force that exists between any two objects, including between the Earth and everything on it
force—an interaction, such as a push or pull, that changes the motion of an object
accelerate—a change in the motion of an object

CONTORTION

A single performer enters the center ring and sits down. The audience waits, curious to see what she will do. She lifts one leg and places it behind her neck. Then she places her other leg behind her neck. She unwraps her legs, leans back, and bends until her head touches the backs of her legs. The audience cheers with each new move.

How does this contortionist bend her body in ways that seem impossible? We use **biomechanics** to explain. Biomechanics uses aspects of physics and biology. Contortionists train their bodies to move beyond the normal physics that apply to human movement. They stretch their muscles and tendons so that they are more elastic and flexible. This gives their joints a wider **range of motion**, which lets them move in unusual ways. Some joints, such as hips and shoulders, can become much more flexible. Others, such as knees and elbows, are much more difficult, if not impossible, to change.

biomechanics—the study of how the human body moves

range of motion—the full movement of a joint, including flexibility and extension

DON'T
TRY THIS AT HOME

TRY THIS INSTEAD

How flexible are you? Sit on the floor with your back against a wall, legs straight out. Now reach toward your toes. How far can you reach? Mark that spot with a piece of tape. Every day, practice this stretch. After a week, measure your reach again and mark the spot. Have you become more flexible?

CIRCUS FACT

Some contortionists also practice enterology. This is the practice of squeezing their bodies into small boxes or other tiny space that seem too small to hold a human.

AERIAL CRADLE

That last act had your heart racing. Can you handle what's next? Suspended above the center ring is what looks like a huge playground swing. Two performers run out from behind the curtain. They scramble up a ladder and onto the seat of the swing. One performer, a flier, stands on the frame above the other performer, the catcher. The catcher hangs from the swing by his knees. The flier leaps and holds on to the catcher's hands. The catcher swings the flier. The audience cheers as the performers carry on.

What is the science behind the aerial cradle? It's all about balance. To stay balanced, the performers must pay close attention to their center of gravity. The center of gravity is the location representing the average position of weight in a body. In other words, it's a body's balancing point. A performer's balancing point must stay directly above the aerial cradle. If she moves her balancing point too much one way or the other, she will begin to fall. Performers learn to make tiny adjustments to their positions so that they can balance in ways that seem impossible.

HORIZONTAL BARS

Four bars, connected in a rectangle, stand about 10 feet (3 meters) off the floor. A performer reaches up and grabs one bar, flipping himself up into a handstand. He swings and leaps to the bar across from him. He goes into another handstand and then does a dizzyingly fast spin. He keeps spinning and spinning and spinning in circles as he holds onto these horizontal bars! Watching him makes you dizzy!

How does this performer keep spinning? He starts each **rotation** in the handstand position at the top of the bar. He must swing down with enough momentum so that he makes it around the bar and back up, overcoming gravity, to reach the top of the bar and start over again. Holding onto the bar is important, particularly at the bottom. As he pulls down on the bar, the bar pushes back and he moves upward. As the performer spins, he has **angular momentum**. As long as he holds the bar with his arms, he swings in a circular path, instead of flying outward.

CIRCUS FACT

This circus act came from the uneven bars that are part of the sport of gymnastics.

rotation—the motion of an object around an internal axis
angular momentum—a measure of an object's rotation, involving mass, shape, and speed

RUSSIAN BAR

This next act is sure to amaze. Two performers, called porters, enter the ring, holding a long bar between them. A third performer, a flier, climbs up onto the bar. She walks across it like a balance beam. The porters then thrust this Russian bar upward, launching the performer into the air. She flips three times. Her feet return to the bar. She lands without falling to the floor. The porters swing the bar from side to side. The flier adjusts her movements to stay balanced.

What's the science behind this amazing circus act? It's all about balance. The flier must know where her center of gravity is. This is the point in her body around which her weight is evenly distributed. The flier only stays balanced on the bar if her center of gravity is directly over it. As the porters move the bar, the flier must move her center of gravity with it. The performers practice their routine again and again. The flier learns to anticipate the movements of the porters so she can quickly adjust her center of gravity.

DON'T TRY THIS AT HOME

TRY THIS INSTEAD

Here is an easy way to experiment with center of gravity and balance. Place a pencil horizontally on your index finger. Find the place where you can balance it. The balancing point should be toward the middle of the pencil. That is its center of gravity. Now try the same thing with an object that is heavier on one end, such as a ballpoint pen or marker with a heavy cap. Where is the center of gravity now? Where did you have to hold it to make it balance on one finger?

CIRCUS FACT

In 2014 Maria Eremina of the Russian Bolshoi Circus was the first person to successfully do a quadruple front somersault on a Russian bar.

FREESTANDING LADDER

A performer carries a ladder into the ring. Can an everyday object like this really make an interesting circus act? You're about to find out! The performer sets the ladder upright. He slowly climbs each rung. Soon he makes it to the top, and swings one leg around so that he's straddling the ladder. He jumps around, remaining on top of the ladder. Then he pulls out rings and juggles. He stays at the top without falling over! You're afraid the ladder will come crashing down, but it doesn't!

It can take a long time for a performer to learn to balance on the freestanding ladder. He begins practicing close to a wall in case he loses his balance and the ladder falls. As the performer climbs each rung, he rocks his body back and forth until he feels stable. The rocking assures his center of gravity, along with the ladder's, remain directly above the ground. Gravity constantly wants to pull the ladder, and the performer, back down. Body strength, and the use of fine muscles, is important in this act. Circus performers with this muscle training can more easily balance.

CIRCUS FACT

Performers on the freestanding ladder also practice falling. Performers must know how to quickly move their position during a fall so they can land in the safest way possible.

GERMAN WHEEL

A performer pushes a huge double wheel into the ring. It looks like two large aluminum hula hoops, connected by crossbars. The performer climbs inside, grabs the wheel with her hands, and braces her feet against the crossbars. Slowly, she starts the wheel turning. She spins with it, going faster and faster. She even goes upside down. Watching her makes you dizzy!

How does the German wheel keep spinning? It uses **gyroscopic motion**. A gyroscope is a wheel spinning along an **axis** that is free to move. An axis is an imaginary line around which an object can spin. Once a gyroscope is spinning, it resists changes to the way it spins. The wheel only stops when a force, such as **friction**, acts to slow it down.

CIRCUS FACT

The German wheel has a relative, the Cyr wheel. A Cyr wheel is a single metal hoop, without crossbars.

gyroscopic motion—the motion characterized by a gyroscope, which is a wheel spinning along an axis that is free to move in any direction
axis—a straight line around which an object rotates
friction—a force that opposes the relative motion of two or more surfaces in contact

CHAIR
STACKING

This last act is really going to bend your mind! Performers carry several chairs into the ring. Are they setting up a game of musical chairs? No. They stack the chairs on top of one another, high into the air. Then one performer carefully climbs to the top. She balances herself on the top chair. Then she breaks out into a handstand! The crowd gasps in awe.

How come this performer, along with the chairs, doesn't come crashing down? The answer is balance. She keeps her center of gravity balanced above the chairs. Also, the transfer of weight is at work. Weight moves from one chair to the next. Putting weight on one part of a chair stack will cause another part to move in the opposite direction. Circus performers must anticipate and work with those reactions to balance the chairs in addition to balancing their weight on them.

There's another trick to this act. Circus chairs may look ordinary, but they are modified to remain stable when stacked. Notches in the legs of the chairs help to hold them in place. The chairs are also weighted in certain spots to help them balance.

DON'T TRY THIS AT HOME

TRY THIS INSTEAD

To see the transfer of weight and balance at work, grab some hardcover books. Place one book so that the spine lines up with the end of a table. Place the second book on top, with the spine sticking out about 1 inch (2.5 cm). Repeat, sticking the next book on top about another 1 inch (2.5 cm) out. How many books can you stack before they start to fall? You can also try stacking them back the other direction and then back out again.

CIRCUS FACT

The record for chair stacking and balancing belongs to Luo Jun of China. He balanced on a stack of 11 chairs.

CIRCUS SAFETY

Did these circus acts totally bend your mind? They are fun to watch, but most circus acts come with some safety risks. Circus performers and other people who work for the circus take every precaution necessary to prevent accidents and injury.

Sometimes safety depends on special equipment. Performers moving high in the air often use rigging. This system of wires and lines keeps the performer from hitting the ground if they fall. Even if rigging isn't used during a show, the performers use it as they learn and practice their acts. Engineers also check equipment often to make sure it is in good shape and will do what it is supposed to do.

Safety is also about being prepared. Performers learn how to fall correctly so that they can minimize injuries. They also practice until they can perform their act safely and confidently. They have an emergency plan if something goes wrong. Spotters watch the acts for any sign of trouble.

angular momentum (ANG-gyu-lur mom-MEN-tuhm)—a measure of an object's rotation, involving mass, shape, and speed

axis (AK-siss)—a straight line around which an object rotates

biomechanics (BY-oh-muh-KA-niks)—the study of how the human body moves

center of gravity (SEN-tur UHV GRAV-uh-tee)—the point in an object around which its weight is evenly distributed

force (FORS)—an interaction that changes the motion of an object

friction (FRIK-shuhn)—a force that opposes the relative motion of two or more surfaces in contact

gravity (GRAV-uh-tee)—an attractive force that exists between any two objects, including between the Earth and everything on it

gyroscopic motion (jy-roh-SKAHP-ick MOH-shun)—the motion characterized by a gyroscope, which is a wheel spinning along an axis that is free to move in any direction

momentum (moh-MEN-tuhm)—a measure of an object's straight-line motion, calculated as a product of its mass and velocity

range of motion (RAYNJ OF MOH-shun)—the full movement of a joint, including flexibility and extension

rotation (roh-TAY-shuhn)—the motion of an object around an internal axis

speed (SPEED)—a measurement of how fast something is moving

weight distribution (WATE dis-tri-BYOO-shun)—the spreading of weight among available supports

READ MORE

Doudna, Kelly. *The Kid's Book of Simple, Everyday Science*. Minneapolis, Minn.: Scarletta, 2013.

Gogerly, Liz. *Circuses. Explore!* London: Wayland, 2017.

Mercer, Bobby. *Junk Drawer Physics: 50 Awesome Experiments that Don't Cost a Thing*. Junk Drawer Science. Chicago: Chicago Review Press, 2014.

Royston, Angela. *Forces and Motion*. Essential Physical Science. Chicago: Heinemann Library, 2014.

Turnbull, Stephanie. *Circus Skills*. Super Skills. Mankato, Minn.: Smart Apple Media, 2013.

INTERNET SITES

Use FactHound to find Internet sites related to this book.

Visit *www.facthound.com*

Just type in 9781515772828 and go.

INDEX